ALONG THE SUSSEX COAST

West Pier, Brighton.

Along the Sussex Coast

Ray Hollands

SUTTON PUBLISHING

Sutton Publishing Limited
Phoenix Mill · Thrupp · Stroud
Gloucestershire · GL5 2BU

First published 2006

Title page photograph: Beachy Head Lighthouse.

British Library Cataloguing in Publication Data
A catalogue record for this book is available from the British Library.

ISBN 0-7509-4063-8

Typeset in 10/12 Gill Sans.
Typesetting and origination by
Sutton Publishing Limited.
Printed in England by
J.H. Haynes & Co. Ltd, Sparkford.

To the memory of Keith Goodyear, who loved the Sussex coast.

While I was standing on the viewing tower of the Visitors' Centre at Littlehampton harbour side, the motor boat obligingly performed an aquatic pirouette complete with a trailing wash.

Contents

While I was walking the perimeter of Bosham Hoe this purposeful landing stage caught my eye, mostly because of its striking length and spindly stick-like supports that were obviously capable of defying the pernicious mud flats on the approach to Bosham Harbour. No doubt many a boarding or disembarking has been made possible by this miniature causeway.

ACKNOWLEDGEMENTS

I should like to thank the following people for their assistance and advice in the preparation of this book: Julie Moore for all her research and for producing the typewritten text; Dr Barry Yates for providing information about the Rye Harbour Nature Reserve; the staff of the Worthing Tourist Information Centre for helpful advice and directions; Teresa and Arthur Speary for their hospitality and eagerness to share their local knowledge; the staff of the Visitor Centre at Cuckmere Haven for information on the area; and Austin Tansley for access to his abundant local knowledge and for pointing me in the right direction, otherwise I might have missed many a photographic opportunity.

This visual cliché was taken at Brighton Beach – the two perennial incumbents await the first takers of the day.

INTRODUCTION

Having decided to explore the coastline of Sussex with a camera, my first resolve was to ensure that I read nothing whatsoever that might give me an insight into the journey. I wanted no preconceived vision of what images I should take or, more to the point, what images 'should' be in a book. That said, I was also aware that inevitably a certain number of well-known landmarks and places were not going to be excluded; no matter how clichéd, their sheer photogenic charm would be enough to fight their corner.

Predictably, this part of the south coast is steeped in history, with its wars and occupations from early Roman and Saxon times through to the Napoleonic threats and culminating in the Second World War; each chapter has left its mark. However, I have tried not to make the book a historical picture show but have followed a west to east direction photographing whatever took my eye as I walked or cycled the county's pathways. All the photographs were taken before attempting any necessary research.

I found it easier to divide the chapters of the book into groups of towns or conurbations, as the coastline did not readily fall into any simple geological areas. On looking at the map this method seemed to present an obvious agenda for the project's contents. It will be noticeable that I have included several locations that are no longer a 'bona fide' part of the coast, Winchelsea being one for example, but their obvious historical and strategic importance in the past I think demands inclusion. One last didactic point! As in my previous Sutton book, *Along the Kent Coast*, I have taken the liberty of including as part of the shoreline any river or inlet that can claim to be tidal and would provide visual interest.

Finally, I hope that this personal anthology of coastal images will not only give enjoyment to the reader (I certainly enjoyed taking them) but encourage some to perhaps visit corners not seen before, or places long overdue a return.

Ray Hollands
2006

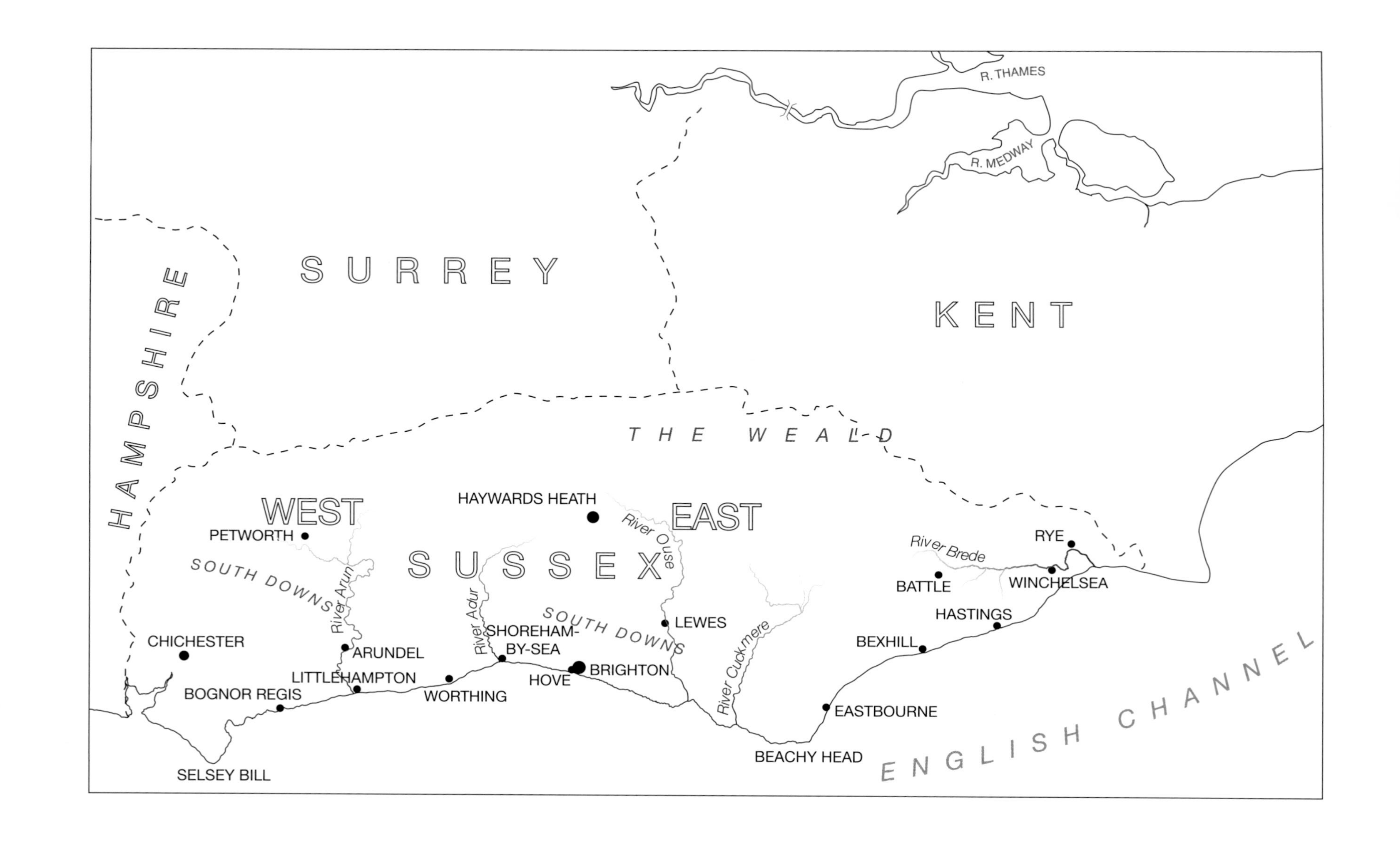
R. THAMES
R. MEDWAY
SURREY
KENT
HAMPSHIRE
THE WEALD
WEST
SUSSEX
EAST
HAYWARDS HEATH
PETWORTH
SOUTH DOWNS
River Arun
River Adur
River Ouse
River Cuckmere
River Brede
RYE
BATTLE
WINCHELSEA
HASTINGS
BEXHILL
LEWES
SHOREHAM-BY-SEA
BRIGHTON
HOVE
WORTHING
ARUNDEL
LITTLEHAMPTON
CHICHESTER
BOGNOR REGIS
SELSEY BILL
EASTBOURNE
BEACHY HEAD
ENGLISH CHANNEL

Chapter One

CHICHESTER, SELSEY BILL & BOGNOR REGIS

CHICHESTER

Chichester is the western limit of the Sussex coast. The Hampshire border runs down the middle of Chichester harbour following the line of the Emsworth Channel. It was the Roman town of Noviomagnus and probably owed its early and rapid development to the pro-Roman king Cogidubnus. Claudius granted Roman citizenship to this British puppet king, who apparently provided a safe haven at Fishbourne for their campaigning in the south-west (see the beautifully preserved mosaic floors at the Fishbourne Roman Palace).

Chichester is basically built on the lines of the standard Roman town with many of the streets following that prescribed pattern. Having the status of a port, despite its quays and wharves being several miles inland, Chichester prospered rapidly during the eighteenth century, enabling its resident affluent merchants to build any number of town houses in Georgian red brick and local flint.

Today the city is modern and vibrant yet without the obligatory frenzy and frustration of most of its busy contemporaries, not least because of the ring road that shunts the wheeled Armageddon away from its centre. The very accessible and walkable cathedral, with its modern outlook and tourist-friendly approach (I saw a sculpture exhibition laid out in its grounds), seems to act as a nucleus, allowing graceful antiquity to interleave with a modern and forward looking culture.

SELSEY BILL

This area is technically an island, as the Broad Rife is a brook running from the mudflats of Pagham harbour to the English Channel at Bracklesham Bay, completing the watery surround. This southern-most point of the Sussex coast has a strong maritime tradition dating back to the seventh century when St Wilfrid allegedly taught his Saxon converts the art of fishing. Today this tradition continues along the East Beach where a sizeable fleet catches a variety of fish, crab and lobster that supply the many pubs and restaurants around the Chichester area.

During the summer months the beach, along with the neighbouring beaches of East and West Wittering, can be inundated with those who desire to be 'beside the sea'. The very best time to walk along the coast (as with all coasts) is in the early morning with the tide out as far as it will go – especially here where there is an incredible light that is brought about by a strip of land that is engulfed by sea.

BOGNOR REGIS

Humble Bognor became Bognor Regis in 1929 after King George V had been advised to convalesce in its healthy climate to recover from a serious operation. Such an accolade inevitably encouraged a growth in numbers of visitors coming to the town; but compared with other south coast resorts Bognor did not really get off the starting block.

The town's prosperity and growth began in the late 1780s when the entrepreneur, Richard Hotham, a London businessman, became aware of the town's marvellous climate and decided to build a health resort to encourage the pampered and affluent to the area. He obviously believed this enterprise would succeed because he built his own house, Hotham Park, with its parkland within the town.

Today it is not the fashionable and affluent that come to the town for their holidays, it is more likely to be a young family staying at the Butlins Resort with its modern creations, such as the huge splash sub-tropical waterworld and twenty-first-century entertainment. There are, of course, miles of wonderful beach and clean sea bathing to enjoy. The sun quota is marginally more than Skelmersdale or Wigan.

Opposite: A serene scene, looking from the East Head across Chichester harbour mouth. The very flatness emphasises its vulnerability. Owned by the National Trust, it is of international importance as an over-wintering haven for a varied population of migrating birds, while at the same time playing a vital role in sheltering the inner reaches of the harbour and being instrumental in protecting the area. It is a fragile environment.

One of the many navigational buoys dotted around Chichester Harbour, a very necessary aid to mariners using the various inlets and channels that make up the harbour complex.

A forest of masts in Chichester Marina. Having taken a boat trip around Chichester Harbour I was amazed by the sheer number of yachts and small craft, mostly bobbing peacefully at anchor. I imagine they are quite a sight when they are all on the move. One salt-tanned boatman I spoke to complained 'that it would soon become as congested as the M25'. He had been sailing here for more than thirty years and had experienced quieter times.

This craft could credibly be described by any number of adjectives: sleek, smooth, cool, even spiffing.

There is much that is inspiring about Chichester Cathedral: a tapestry by John Piper, a painting by Graham Sutherland and a stunning Marc Chagall window as well as several twelfth-century sculptures. Work began on the Cathedral in about 1080, the intention being to replace the Saxon one at Selsey that was being threatened by the encroaching sea. Its medieval origins have undergone a good number of renewals and refurbishments over the years; the well-known spire, visible from land and sea, was not itself built until 1866. Here it is shown in early morning light with the sun just catching the flint wall of the closure.

This is generally a peaceful scene but absolute bliss early on a summer's morning. The two canal boats, the *Richmond* and the *Egremont*, wait quietly in the still waters of the canal basin for the day's work to begin. Trips from the basin to the village of Hunston and back are provided by the Chichester Ship Canal Trust, which is manned by the 'friends' of the Trust, each one a volunteer. There are plans to open the stretch of canal between Hunston and Chichester Marina, thereby directly linking the city of Chichester to the sea once again.

Bosham Harbour – one of the most-painted, most-photographed scenes in Britain – is a veritable stockpile of history. It was here that King Cnut allegedly commanded the incoming tide to turn back – a useful skill indeed, for I am told that at certain times when there is an exceptional tide many of the roads around the harbour are subjected to flooding. It was from here that Godwin's son Harold departed on his ill-fated expedition to Normandy. The rest as they say is history. The chancel arch of Bosham church is depicted in the Bayeux Tapestry for posterity.

This scene of tranquillity belies the fact that in the seventeenth and eighteenth centuries Dell Quay was probably the busiest commercial port in the whole of Sussex, exporting wheat, barley and wool, and importing wine and salt from the continent and coal from Newcastle.

Described by Arthur Mee (King's England series, Sussex volume) as 'perhaps the smallest port in England, a house or two, a shed or two, a small jetty', the port's commercial career had come to a virtual standstill by the 1940s. Today the quay is home to Chichester Harbour Conservancy Education Centre and proudly boasts a new pontoon (funded by Heritage Lottery money), allowing easy boarding to the solar-powered classroom, 'Solar Heritage'.

Opposite: 'His and Hers.' The boatyard at West Itchenor, where there has long been a tradition of boatbuilding and maintenance. The title is mere fancy and wishful thinking.

Standing like sentries on duty is this line of posts along the narrow spit of sand and dunes that connects the East Head with West Wittering. Beneath this strip of land, known as the Hinge, is a rock berm which has been installed on the seaward side of the strip in hope of preventing a breach that would form a new tidal channel. Unfortunately, there had been a breaching at the end of 2004 and previously in 1963. Efforts to prevent a permanent tidal channel being created are at present being hampered by the conflicting priorities of the various agencies involved. Attempts to reach an agreement and thereby produce a solution could possibly lead to a public enquiry.

These are the fragile dunes of the East Head at West Wittering with their waving grasses and sunny hollows. Beware of hot summer days when the area can become inundated with the ubiquitous sun worshipper and this empty almost desolate image would seem to be a lie. The National Trust own and manage this unique little spot, but one can't help thinking that it is not an easy task.

This early morning shot of the beach at Selsey reminded me of the paintings by Edward Hopper, a distillation of loneliness and sought-after isolation. The unusual rooftop to the right of the picture focuses the eye away from the deserted beach. Who lives there? What do they do? We have no idea about lifestyles or personalities because there are no visible points of reference from which to make a judgement. A reclusive cult film director or a retired inspector of urban sewers?

Selsey Bill Lifeboat Station looking justly important as it stretches out into the sea.
When I first saw it I could not help thinking that the access ramp looked nearly as long as Bognor Pier.

Pagham Harbour is a tidal basin that has long since ceased to be of any commercial importance; the sea last broke through what could have been considered the harbour back in 1910 and no attempt to reinstate this facility has been made since. However, it has become recognised as an internationally important wetland for many breeding species of birds as well as a migratory haven.
During the Middle Ages it was apparently a workable harbour, but by the mid-fourteenth century the sea had breached the defences and completely flooded the area. There were attempts during the nineteenth century at reinstatement and reclamation of the land for agricultural purposes, but to no avail.
Today the site is managed by West Sussex County Council, which looks after over 200 breeds of birds, more than 340 types of flowering plants, over 280 species of moth and 13 different species of woodlice – incredible! However, during the peak of the migration period it is said that it is possible to spot more 'twitchers' than all the birds, moths, flowers and woodlice put together.

Just after sunrise, looking across Pagham Harbour from a point near the site of the old Sidlesham ferry. At one time this point was the crossing from Selsey Island to the mainland, not by road but by ferry-boat at high tide and the 'Wadeway' at low tide. It was not until 1932 that the present causeway was constructed, which raised the land enough to eventually allow the B2145 to be built.

This rather sterile scene of Pagham Harbour early in the morning and at low tide rather belies the fact that it is amazingly alive. This salt marsh with its huge deposits of soft mud and unique plants that can survive this extremely salty environment is home to a complex ecosystem. The leaves of the plants rot down to add nutrition to the already fertile mud soup upon which myriads of tiny creatures find sustenance, both from the rotting leaves and the continued flowing tide of bacteria from land and sea. This also sustains crabs, snails, shrimps and any number of worms, which in turn provide food for thousands of wildfowl and waders that over-winter here before returning to their Arctic home.

I imagine that this large clump of teasels had been cultivated by the harbour nature reserve – I have never seen such numbers as this before – to encourage seed-eating birds such as finches. They make a glorious sight with the sun just rising behind them.

This is believed to be a piece of a Mulberry harbour left over from the Second World War. The name Mulberry was derived from the codename of the engineering operation that produced two of these artificial floating harbours, created for the Allied invasion of Normandy in 1944. These ingenious structures were prefabricated in England, towed across the Channel and sunk into position along the French coast, allowing troops and equipment to disembark whatever the state of the tide.

What a pity that this fitting memorial to the bravery and ingenuity of those involved in the Allied landings of 1944 should fall prey to mindless vandalism.

Walking eastwards along the shore from Pagham is not a particularly exciting journey – pleasant but repetitive – until you see the closely compacted beach groynes with Bognor's pier mirror-imaged in the far distance.

Keeping Cool In Bognor. At a quick glance the dogs could be mistaken for sheep, but I doubt if their owners would be mistaken for shepherds.

Unfortunately, not all of Bognor's seafront is quite as elegant as this Edwardian bandstand, which displays a fine example of strut work that supports the roof and is typical of the period. Sadly, the same cannot be said about the pier seen in the background.

Opposite: I found this delightful drinking fountain sitting obdurately on the seafront at Bognor. Totally unexpected, it is an anachronism among the usual rock shops, fish restaurants and ice cream kiosks. It reminded me of the now nearly extinct horse troughs that often had a drinking fountain alongside them; the trouble was you were never quite sure which one the horse had been drinking out of!

Poor Bognor Pier! It is one of the oldest in Britain and is beginning to look its age. Originally it was 1,000ft long, but bits keep dropping off. The pavilion at the end sank in 1965 and more was swept away in a storm in 1999. Even on the day that I set off to photograph it, a blinding summer's day, a sea mist fell within minutes from nowhere, presenting a hauntingly sad image.

From a distance the town of Arundel always looks as though it has been piled up atop the hill, in the same way that children pile up pebbles on the beach. My favourite view is across the river looking from the east where one sees none of the modern trappings of today – just the river, the trees and the castle. Built in 1067 by Richard of Montgomery and passing to the Duke of Norfolk in the mid-sixteenth century, the castle has been in the same family ever since. It is not without its aesthetic detractors (because of its fanciful restoration), but I have always found it to be a stunningly exciting view when it first comes into sight.

It is difficult to believe that not so long ago Stopham's medieval bridge was still carrying traffic over the River Arun (still tidal at this point), facilitated by a set of traffic lights. Pedestrians negotiated the precarious task of crossing by dodging into the recesses on the bridge parapet. Early in the nineteenth century the central arch was raised to enable more northerly navigation for the transportation of coal and corn about the area, but apart from that the bridge remains remarkably as it was in the fifteenth century. I can only imagine that it has to be one of the finest examples in the whole country.

Chapter Two

LITTLEHAMPTON, WORTHING & SHOREHAM

LITTLEHAMPTON

This is a town that seems to have reinvented itself. Once Henry VIII's Royal Dockyard, the town has maintained a tradition of boatbuilding up to the present day. Boatbuilding activity is still to be found on the west side of the river; over 100 lifeboats were built during the second half of the twentieth century. Paradoxically, Littlehampton Lifeboat Station had been closed in 1921 – but an appeal on TV by the children's programme *Blue Peter* raised enough public money for a new, powerful, inflatable rescue boat, and the lifeboat station was reopened in 1967. Who remembers the programme's appeal? I certainly do.

Today the town boasts a clean and safe beach area for the whole family to enjoy, the shore and harbour mouth being patrolled by a team of life guards throughout the summer. Upriver towards the footbridge, where once there would have been steam packets departing for France, the area has undergone a tasteful face-lift offering a choice of riverside shops, pubs and restaurants. There is an imaginative and pleasant visitor centre by the river – 'the Look and Sea' – presenting the opportunity to take in the splendid scenery from its viewing tower, perhaps even a photograph or two!

WORTHING

Having recently read William Newton's charming book *The Two Pound Tram*, I half expected my meanderings along the Worthing seafront to evoke reminiscences of the bygone era that he captures so marvellously. I didn't even see a dog that remotely resembled Tiger – a prominent character in the book: perhaps the Dome cinema came close to capturing the bygone age that the author wrote about.

Like many seaside resorts Worthing started life as a small fishing village. Its potential to become fashionable was raised considerably when Princess Amelia, sister of the future

Prince Regent, visited in 1798. The resort became popular with the fashionable and wealthy who believed that 'taking the waters' was the panacea to all their various ills. In today's world that probably equates to imbibing alcopops in the night club at the end of the pier.

Despite modern redevelopment over the years Worthing still retains considerable architectural wealth, Park Crescent by Amon Wilds (*c.* 1830) being a prime example and Liverpool Terrace with its sinuous bays another. If promenading is your scene, and it still appears to be extremely popular, then there is probably no better place to indulge your passion than along the Worthing Prom – its up-to-date planting, including palm trees, have given it a real feel of the Mediterranean.

SHOREHAM

Travelling east from Worthing you come upon the sprawling ribbon of water that is Shoreham Harbour, not one that readily suggests poetic thoughts. Like most sea ports along this part of the coast its history has been dictated by siltings, widening and continuous dredgings. In the 1950s an improved enlargement of the lock ensured the sustainability of the port's commercial future. Today the harbour comfortably caters for both the needs of its mercantile shipping and the leisure craft that co-exist along its waters. Fortunately, the town of New Shoreham (founded in about 1100 AD by William de Braose) is situated to the west of the dockside quays and wharves, so one is not too frequently reminded of the commercial grittiness of a working port, particularly when away from the pleasant but traffic-noisy High Street, where just to the north stands the magnificent Church of St Mary de Haura and its quiet surroundings.

Opposite: These moorings on the west bank of the river at Littlehampton have definitely seen better times. However, from a photographer's point of view their down-at-heel condition exhibits a wonderful variety of textures and gives the scene an edgy atmosphere. I doubt waxing lyrical would impress the owner of the boat who must take his life in his hands, or at least risk a soaking, each time he boards his craft. I thought walking the plank had ceased to be legal!

Littlehampton still maintains a thriving boatbuilding business; the skills that once supported a royal dockyard have not deserted it. These hapless creatures could do with a little TLC though: the maintenance queue must have been longer than an NHS waiting list.

As can be seen from this photograph most of the harbour is taken up with leisure craft and a small fishing fleet; much of the busy sea trade that used the harbour in earlier times has dwindled dramatically. The main shipping trade is now involved with the dredging of sand and shingle from the seabed; the days when the steam packets would ply their trade have long since disappeared. Sadly, the only evidence today that Littlehampton operated as a passenger port is the Steam Packet Public House that stands by the quayside, opposite the boatyards, a reminder of times when travel had a quite different and more sedate complexion.

Taking coffee on the harbour walk at Littlehampton. Just as the textures on page 41 caught my eye, so I was attracted to the patterns in this shot.

Opposite: Worthing Pier, designed by Sir Robert Rawlinson and built at a cost of around £6,500, was officially opened on 12 April 1862. The building of piers was very fashionable in the nineteenth century and Worthing's was an immediate success. Because of its popularity a pavilion was opened in 1889 at the far end of the pier. A new landing stage enabled paddle steamers to moor off its southern end. Quickly becoming popular with visitors and locals alike, this novel and pleasurable activity was epitomised by the famous *Worthing Belle*.

Heavy seas and gale-force winds hit the pier on Easter Monday 1913, washing away part of the decking linking it to the shore. The detached pavilion became known as Easter Island. Not content to sit back and lick its wounds, Worthing had completed the repair work and reopened the pier by May 1914; it was opened by none other than the Lord Mayor of London.

The pier's troubles, however, were far from over. On 10 September 1933 the south pavilion was destroyed by fire. Yet again, with resolute determination, the pier was again reopened within two years, only to be confronted with another trauma a few years later. At the outbreak of war in 1939 the whole south coast was on major alert as a prime target for possible invasion; one preventative measure apparently necessitated the blowing of a 120ft hole in the south end of the pier. Today, strolling along the deck in the sunshine, it is difficult to imagine that this pleasant, relaxed promontory has undergone such a beleaguered history. A very prescient quote on a leaflet from the Visitor Centre says it all: 'Blown Down, Burnt Down, Blown Up'.

I took this photograph of Worthing seafront because I thought that the palm trees gave it the look of the Mediterranean.

In the centre of the photograph can be seen Worthing's famous Dome cinema, a unique example of an Edwardian leisure centre. It was originally known as a Kursaal: this German word described a building that housed several forms of entertainment under one roof, sometimes accompanied by a fashionable spa. It was one Carl Seebold, a Swiss man, who presented the idea of a Kursaal to the town of Worthing. The development of the building followed several stages, beginning with Pleasure Gardens and an open-air theatre. On Easter Sunday 1911 a large rectangular hall was opened: it was designed by Theodophilus Allen and very soon introduced the popular pastime of roller skating. A little later another form of entertainment was opened on the upper floor – moving pictures.

Further developments included upholstered, tip-up armchairs, cloakrooms, refreshment rooms and a tower. At the outbreak of the First World War the provider of this wonderful new amenity felt obliged to change the name of the Kursaal to that of the Dome. Anti-German feeling in the town also persuaded him to drop his middle name – Adolf.

Between the wars and indeed right up to the 1990s the Dome endured mixed fortunes; fortunately a local pressure group, Save The Dome, appears to have rescued it from demolition. Fittingly, now a Grade II listed building, the Dome operates two screens on the site of the original 1911 Electric Theatre.

A groyne on Worthing Beach.

The Pavilion Theatre was built on the northern end of Worthing pier in 1926, in an Edwardian/Baroque style that forms an impressive frontage to the pier entrance. Built originally as a concert hall with the intention of attracting the wealthy to move to Worthing, today it provides a wide variety of entertainment catering for all tastes.

Opposite: This delightful, almost toy town airport presents an impression of what it was like to travel by air in the leisurely 1930s. Designed by Stavers Hessell Tiltman, building started on the art deco project in October 1934. It was opened on 13 June 1936 by a trio of mayors from Brighton, Hove and Worthing. The interior of the building still contains many of its original 1930s features. This Grade II listed building is open to the public, offering a licensed bar and restaurant, a museum and visitor centre and occasional guided tours of the airport itself. This working building can be enjoyed by any that have a feeling for design in the art deco style.

SHOREHAM (BRIGHTON CITY) AIRPORT
WARNING

This Dutch-like seascape was taken from the busy Norfolk Bridge on the outskirts of Shoreham. Up the river is a rail bridge and beyond that the Old Shoreham Toll Bridge, with Lancing College in the background.

Opposite: This delightful church sits in the peaceful backwater of Old Shoreham – only just out of earshot of the nearby A27 and a little upriver of the hectic Norfolk bridge. If one has travelled either of these roads in busy traffic, to pull off the road and bask in the tranquillity of this little Norman church is akin to coming upon an oasis in the middle of a desert. The oldest parts of St Nicholas's Church date back to the Saxon period, that is pre-900 AD, and are situated at the western end of the building. They include a tower and the nave. The north and south transepts and the central tower are all Norman; the rest is of more modern construction.

Old Shoreham and its toll bridge seem like a well-kept secret between the bustle of the A27 and the congested A259 – a frame from the past left behind by time and tide. It is difficult to believe that this was the main highway over the River Adur between Brighton and Portsmouth, even used by double-decker buses right up until it was closed to traffic in 1968. Before it was built in 1781 people and animals were pulled across the estuary on a flat raft; one can imagine a Constable setting with farm folk and animals blissfully traversing the river on a summer's day. Today this Grade II listed site, with its twenty-eight trestles spanning the river, is still used by walkers, cyclists and horse riders. Sadly, though, it is in need of considerable restoration.

A close-up of the Old Shoreham toll bridge with a swan emerging from between its ancient trestles.

Looking across the River Adur to the magnificent church of St Mary de Haura, New Shoreham. This giant church with its great tower dominating almost every view of the town was built to serve New Shoreham after the silting of the harbour at Old Shoreham. The church that we see today is only half the original size; it is said that the first patron, Philip de Braose, envisaged a monastery to celebrate his return from the Crusades in 1103. It is rare in its mixture of Norman and Transitional styles and is a fine example of how Norman eased into Gothic, showing motifs of these contrasting designs in the one building.

Chapter Three

BRIGHTON & HOVE

BRIGHTON

In some ways more sedate than Eastbourne and in other ways more vulgar than Blackpool, Brighton has a vibrant paradoxical mix that has helped it to become arguably the most popular seaside resort in Britain. Cultural and comfortably cosmopolitan, it is known as 'London by the sea'. The more critical, however, suggest that 'Croydon by the sea' would be more apt. Whatever one's opinion of current and past developments it is difficult to deny the liveliness and undiminished popularity of the area: residential and business properties are eagerly sought after by high- and low-profile celebrities alike as well as the rest of us. A council injection of around £40 million for improvement and regeneration of the city has no doubt given great encouragement to several planned development projects, notably Sir Terence Conran's restoration of a Grade II listed art deco apartment building.

The seaside resort of Brighton developed from much humbler origins. Moving to a small fishing village (then called Brighthelmstone), a Dr Richard Russell was convinced (he at least convinced the wealthy) of the medicinal values of fresh sea air combined with the unusual habit of jumping into the 'briny' – seabathing became popular and so did little Brighthelmstone. Some trusting folk were even encouraged to drink small quantities of the stuff for the benefit of their health; whether this proved effective was of little consequence, for Brighton was on the road to fame and prosperity.

Royal patronage greatly encouraged and endorsed its popularity; the first royal visitors were George III's brothers, the Dukes of Gloucester, York and Cumberland. The Prince of Wales, later the Prince Regent and George IV, first stayed in Brighton in 1783. His presence greatly influenced its popularity and subsequent development. He took a house in the town after secretly marrying Maria FitzHerbert, a Catholic, which was not the smartest constitutional move, although modern-day digressions of protocol have proved equally problematic.

In 1815 John Nash, the architect, was engaged to build a pleasure dome, the Royal Pavilion, possibly the most incongruous but most-loved royal edifice in the land. Brighton's reputation and the 'wannabe' fashionable had arrived and taken residence, and their influence has shaped the town to the present day.

Brighton continues to flourish. With easy access to London, it is a natural choice for commuters, attracting young professionals and media types who reflect its cosmopolitan atmosphere. For the visitor there is the beach, the Pavilion, one-and-a-bit piers and the vibrant buzz of its celebrated night life. Those less nocturnally inclined can enjoy the fascination of the old town, with its brick-paved lanes and alleyways known as 'The Lanes', which present a mix of fashionable boutiques and specialist shops and a liberal smattering of pubs and restaurants laid out as if in a medieval pattern.

This is a place of change and progress. Once graced by a Prince Regent; later benignly terrorised by Mods and Rockers, immortalised by Graham Greene in *Brighton Rock*; now to some extent colonised by young careerists seeking a rest from the pressures of London. Why not Brighton?

HOVE

Hove to the west is rather shy and retiring compared with its more flamboyant sibling, boasting quiet (except for the traffic) sumptuous squares and terraces. An architectural boundary exists between the two; accompanied by a pace of life that is slower, timely, less congested and without the frenzy that is egotistical Brighton. However, there are ambitious proposed schedules of development for this area too. The large and significant King Alfred Project is to be designed by Frank Gehry, famous for the Bilbao Guggenheim Museum, to create a mixed leisure and residential facility that is expected to attract nearly 1 million more visitors to the area.

A quiet moment for the lifeguards along the beach at Hove. Like the lifeboat and coastguard services they offer considerable reassurance so that the rest of us can enjoy our leisure pursuits with a certain peace of mind.

Both Brighton and Hove have much fine architecture that is still unspoilt by more recent additions or redevelopments. However, to photograph some of the finer examples without the inclusion of rows of motor cars or peripatetic forests of scaffolding is almost impossible. I took pleasure in nearly succeeding with this building.

Brighton Pier was arguably the first pier ever built; this 1,722ft long structure is the most well-known and loved attraction on the south coast. It was hauntingly featured in the film of the Graham Greene novel *Brighton Rock*, with the wonderful photography of Harry Waxman evoking a memorable *noir* atmosphere to the whole setting.

In 1891 work commenced on a new pier (Palace Pier) to replace the original Chain Pier; designed by Richard St George Moore, it opened in May 1899. Although it experienced a golden age during the 1920s and '30s, it reopened in 1946 to enjoy a new lease of life. During the Second World War the pier suffered the indignity of having its mid-section removed to prevent the possibility of an invasion force using the pier to its advantage.

Since being acquired by the Noble Organisation in the mid-1980s the pier has undergone extensive renovation and adopted a more contemporary approach to its attractions and facilities, developing amusements and entertainments that cater for a wide spectrum of tastes. Gone are the mechanical cranes of the penny arcade days, where the polished claws allowed the packet of five Woodbines to slip irretrievably at the very last second; instead one can while away the time with the latest computer games. There are bars and restaurants and modern shopping outlets, all of which helped to win the accolade of Pier of the Year in 1996.

Today the pier has attained the status of a Grade II listed building. Impressively it retains a relaxed and 'fun-at-the-seaside' atmosphere, providing many facilities and considerable free entertainment, as well as an enjoyable stroll on a summer's day.

This unique little kiosk on Brighton pier was at the time of the photograph trading in personal horoscopes and fortune-telling. For a long time it had been the entrance booth to the pier itself and has changed its function a good many times, as it will probably continue to do in the future. Hopefully, its unique and individual design will ensure its preservation for many years to come.

Part of the permanent fairground on Brighton Pier. I waited patiently for this shot, missing it on a couple of occasions, but it very soon became apparent that most of the riders were Japanese – they seem to have a greater than average delight in scaring themselves silly. I would have spent my five tokens in a much more judicious manner.

Designed by Eugenius Birch, West Pier was opened in 1863 as a promenade deck, stealing the glory from the old Chain Pier (something new, something better) only to have its own thunder stolen by the newer Palace Pier built on the site of the old Chain Pier.

The career of the West Pier has been a varied one. First it was damaged by wreckage from the old Chain Pier that had been severely hit by a storm in 1896. Then part of the pier was converted to a theatre in 1903 and an amusement arcade was added in 1945. The pier closed on 30 September 1975, not making a newsworthy ripple until the violent storms of December 2002 that were thought by many to have announced its demise. Controversy rampaged, however, with one group fighting for its restoration and survival and others believing that it would be prudent to allow nature to take its course. Subsequent events made the decision academic. A fire on 28 March 2003 engulfed the south end of the pier structure; another in May 2003 left only the framework standing. If that was not enough a storm on 24 June 2004 caused further structural damage. The pier has been photographed more times in the last three years of its life than it has ever been since 1863!

Looking a bit like a sad old fighter who has gone on a little too far past his sell-by date! This photograph of the West Pier at Brighton, taken from the Palace Pier, would seem to confirm its irrefutable demise. No more letters of outrage in the local newspaper; no more 'save the pier' groups fired by inviolable determination; no more fervent cries for restoration. The old thing lies broken and done for, quietly waiting for a last act of kindness – demolition.

This splendid piece of bizarre architecture is as famous as the nearby Palace Pier. The Pavilion was built as a Regency palace serving as home to three monarchs and always appearing distinctly incongruous set among its surroundings. It is a masterpiece of extravaganza with all the flamboyancy of the man (George IV, at the time Prince Regent) who commissioned John Nash to redesign the less exotic and far humbler formal palace that it once had been. Indian and Chinese influences prevail with what appear to be traces of Moorish and Gothic elements thrown in for good measure. The Prince Regent and his new building certainly had a hand in forever changing the peaceful seaside village into the busy and fashionable resort that we know today.

Nash started work on redesigning the palace in 1815, completing the work in 1822 and altering Brighton's skyline in the most exotic and unfamiliar way. The Pavilion has experienced a somewhat chequered career; in 1850, finding the building less to her liking, Queen Victoria decided to sell it to the local council for a mere £53,000 – it had allegedly cost upwards of £750,000 to build. During the First World War it was used as a hospital for wounded servicemen; the inter-war years saw a decline in its condition, until 1945 when a newly formed Regency society undertook the initiative for its restoration. However, its problems had not ended; there was a fire in 1975 and in the 1987 hurricane a minaret was sent crashing through the dome to the floor beneath. Today it is business as usual once again.

This photograph of the western arm of Brighton Marina demonstrates its construction. Massive reinforced caissons weighing some 600 tons each were made up on site and were subsequently put in place by an enormous crane that itself had to be constructed here. Work had begun on the marina in 1971, and the last caisson was put into place at the end of the east breakwater in 1976, but the pathway to completion was marred when the original budget was dangerously exceeded.

In 1985 the Brent Walker company took over the Marina, spearheaded by the flamboyant personality of businessman George Walker, brother of the famous British World Heavyweight boxing hope Billy Walker. George had been a boxer himself but obviously felt more comfortable bobbing and weaving in the cut and thrust of the business world. George Walker's initiative saw the development of a village in the centre of the complex, with shops and restaurants and later residential properties that were an integral part of the inner harbour. Today the marina village is a town within a town.

Opposite: These two shots were taken from virtually the same spot, proving the fact that while the Brighton Marina is predominantly given over to leisure craft, the commercial fishing trade still manages to survive alongside more affluent neighbours. One imagines that, except for having the sea beneath their feet, the owners of the two different crafts live in worlds that are light years apart.

This charming black smock mill sits on Beacon Hill adjacent to the A259 at Rottingdean. Surrounded by grassland and a putting green, it gracefully overlooks the busy Brighton Road; for the frustrated motorist heading to or from work it must be a pertinent reminder of more bucolic times. Erected in 1802, it ceased to be a working mill in the early 1880s, and by 1890 was even considered for demolition. The land on which it stood was owned by the Marquess of Abergavenny and it was he who, in 1905, undertook the work of major renovation. Today it is cared for by the Rottingdean Preservation Society.

Opposite: Looking east across the arm of Brighton Marina to where the seaside of the promontory is littered with what appears to be hundreds of pieces of a jigsaw puzzle. It would be interesting to know how the design for this sea defence mechanism came about.

The harbour is just as much the hub of the town of Newhaven today as it was in the past. Once a shipping port that dealt with oak from the Weald, wines and spirits from the Continent and slab ice from the Baltic, it plays just as diverse a role today. The cross-Channel ferry service provides a busy link with the Continent and the harbour supports an active fishing fleet as well as offering good facilities to yachtsmen, divers, anglers and most water-sports enthusiasts.

Much of the surrounding area is littered with defensive works from different periods of Newhaven's historic past – many from the Second World War when the town was a prime target. The photograph was taken from the old fort (now a museum) on the west hill overlooking the town and harbour.

Chapter Four

EASTBOURNE & BEACHY HEAD

EASTBOURNE

Eastbourne can legitimately claim to be one of the sunniest places in the country, often top of the sunshine league table; it is absolutely ideal for seaside bandstand entertainment and gentle promenading. But it can proudly boast more.

Before 1850 it was a small, inland, rural village, until a rail line was opened up in 1849 along with a significant increase in development at the nearby hamlet of Southbourne. A seaside resort was emerging. A local landowner and entrepreneur, the Earl of Burlington, embarked on an enterprising programme of building, the Regency-style Burlington Hotel along the seafront being the most notable of the period. Early architectural tastes favoured this style that had begun in Brighton, but as the town began to grow and newcomers with varying tastes and pockets arrived so did fresh styles.

A more modern but equally ambitious development is the marina to the east of the town. Opened in 1993, the Sovereign Harbour project is the largest composite mooring in the UK with over 600 permanent berths and upwards of 3,000 visiting yachts annually. The outer harbour is tidal and the remaining four harbours (Inner, South, North and West) are accessed by two large locks manned continuously by Sovereign Harbour staff. The complex includes pubs, shops, restaurants and an expanding residential development.

BEACHY HEAD

To the West lies the most famous feature of the South Downs, Beachy Head, the tallest sea cliff in Britain (500ft) of dazzling white chalk and glinting flint. Here it is as if you are on top of the world, the sheer vertical white mass beneath your feet offering magnificent panoramic views from the unfenced cliff edge. Unfortunately, as well as the scenic opportunities there is the tragedy of the many incidents that occur from this splendid viewpoint. Apparently, on a very clear day it is just possible to make out Dungeness power station in Kent to the east and the outline of the Isle of Wight to the west – not too many beauty spots can offer such grand vistas!

The base of the cliff face near Cuckmere Haven could be a dry-stone wall. From this photograph it is easy to see how cliff falls are brought about; this erosion at sea level will guarantee that the cliff above will fall in time. Apparently, thousands of years ago a form of loess was driven by Arctic winds and deposited on top of the chalk cliff. This covering of loess, mixed with rain, formed an acid solution that slowly permeated down through tiny channels in the chalk, eating away and widening the fissures, until a karstland type of block formation is completed as seen in the photograph. The sea and heavy rainfall do the rest.

Undoubtedly one of the most interesting and attractive scenes along the Sussex coast, the Seven Sisters was formed some 140 million years ago when the sea sliced through the soft chalk to leave the splendid cliff line that we see today, situated at the point where the South Downs meet the English Channel. This major conservation area is maintained by the Sussex Downs Conservation Board which offers access to a park of nearly 700 acres and an excellent visitors' centre; other facilities include a canoe centre, cycle hire, educational facilities and restaurant.

The Seven Sisters looking west from Birling Gap with Seaford Head in the distance. Birling Gap has suffered dramatically over the last few decades from cliff erosion, where houses have had to be abandoned and eventually surrendered to the sea. The cliffs are eroding at a rate of up to 3ft per year. Most falls of the soft chalk are the direct result of rough seas or heavy rain. Both the owners (National Trust) and the government appear to have adopted a 'laissez-faire' attitude and seem content to allow nature to take its course, which in some ways seems to be the correct stance.

This neatly moored fishing boat at Birling Gap is not the result of an act of mindless vandalism but one of necessity. The sea, like a terrier, is forever snapping at the base of the vertical cliff and the dwelling looks close enough to be approaching the precarious. If the boat was kept on level ground (as I imagine it sometimes has to be) access to the sea would be difficult and dangerous. A wonderful combination of compromise and enterprise.

This precarious tower of crumbling chalk near Beachy Head stands like an ancient cathedral prepared for the inevitable. In another setting it could easily be mistaken for the remains of a wall of a fifteenth-century church or abbey. I rather imagine that the ruin of a medieval church will remain standing long after this has fallen into the sea below. Looking at the detail of the picture it is easy to believe that certain lumps are ready to fall should a slightly overweight dog run by on the cliff top above.

Opposite: 50° 44'.0 N 00° 14'.50 E. This is the exact position of the Beachy Head Lighthouse. This famous lighthouse is probably the best known in England, standing 140ft high and approximately 500ft from the base of the cliffs out into the sea. Earlier lighthouses had been sited on the top of the cliff but were abandoned because of frequent cliff falls or blankets of mist obscuring the light signal. Established in 1828, electrified in 1960 and automated in 1983, this distinctive lighthouse has a range of 25 nautical miles.

The Normans knew the impressive beach head cliff as the *beau chef* – beautiful headland; but beneath this impressive promontory was a graveyard for ships. Not until the 1830s, however, was it thought necessary to light this hazard when the Belle Toute, a cliff top lighthouse, was built to the west of where the current one stands today. Belle Toute was abandoned in 1899, partly because its light was so often obscured by mist and because of its general inadequacy as a navigational beacon. Apparently, it can be rented as a self-catering holiday home. Great if you don't mind heights and have no fear of cliff falls in the night!

Eastbourne is not only renowned for its record-breaking hours of sunlight, but also for its child-friendly environment, as this photograph shows; it even supplies cuddly little pets for the paddling pool. No doubt this 'sweetie' will have put on a little weight by the end of the school holidays!

There is a definite genre of seaside architecture, especially relating to small buildings and most noticeably kiosks; their quaintness and quirkiness are designed specifically to catch the eye. This kiosk on Eastbourne seafront, with the pier in the background, epitomises the style perfectly. Unfortunately, the notice on the left-hand side of the fascia happens to be a police notice seeking information regarding a recent seafront murder.

Like most piers, Eastbourne's was built basically as a promenade, with half a dozen or so small kiosks and a tollboothed entrance. More sophisticated attractions, such as the camera obscura and pavilion, were later additions. Opened by Lord Edward Cavendish on 13 June 1870, it was not actually completed for a further two years. It was yet another design by the popular Eugenius Birch, incorporating an innovative procedure that placed the superstructure supports on specially designed cups set on the rock-bed, the same way that heavy furniture is placed in cups to prevent damage to the carpet. This ingenious concept would allow a certain amount of movement of the structure in bad weather. The theory was obviously fairly sound because over the next 100 years or so, despite the most unfriendly weather conditions typical of the south coast, Eastbourne pier has survived very well.

The pier's camera obscura has not been quite so resilient. Built in 1901, it was at the time the largest in the country. However, during the Second World War it was almost destroyed to prevent it falling into enemy hands – a fact that confuses me! Nevertheless, it was restored at the end of the war, only in 1970 to once more suffer retirement after a fire destroyed the access ways to the camera housing. Restoration to the Dome has now been completed and the 'dark chamber' is now open for business.

'Oh, I Do Like to be Beside the Seaside!' The British penchant for brass bands and seaside bandstands is part of the collective fabric of what it is to be British. Seaside bandstand music continues to thrive, and even if you are not an ardent supporter it is always uplifting, on a summer's day, to catch the distant throb of a band in full swing as its sounds waft lazily towards you. I photographed this lonely Eastbourne bandstand in spring time. Its iridescent dome and golden finial lend the building a certain majesty. Built in the early 1930s, the bandstand succeeded a previous one built in 1893. Interestingly, there is a commemorative plaque at the rear of the current bandstand in memory of an Eastbourne bandsman, John Wesley Woodward, who was playing on the *Titanic* when it went down on 15 April 1912.

Separate Tables – a play by Terence Rattigan?
No – Eastbourne seafront before the visitors arrive!

Sovereign Harbour is the largest man-made marina complex in the UK. Built at the eastern end of the town, its leisure and residential facilities still appear to be expanding, despite being in its twelfth year. The photograph provides little evidence of the busy, bustling yacht haven that is the reality, but looks east across the harbour mouth to an old Martello tower with what, unfortunately, appears to be a modern look-out construction sitting upon it.

This page and overleaf: The somewhat idyllic setting belies the importance and historical drama that has surrounded this skeleton of a castle. Pevensey Castle, one of the largest built by the Romans in southern England, was designed to defend the port against continued invasion by the Saxon hordes. In 1066 William the Conqueror landed his invasion force at the port of Pevensey and most likely sheltered his troops here before marching out to meet King Harold in the famous battle. Most of what is left to see today was built by William's brother, Robert de Mortain, using the earlier Roman wall as a first line of defence and incorporating a deep moat around the keep in the usual Norman fashion. Today the castle sits peacefully half a mile from the sea behind the drained levels of Pevensey.

Chapter Five

HASTINGS & BEXHILL-ON-SEA

HASTINGS

This is another Sussex town generously steeped in history. What schoolchild has not heard of the Battle of Hastings, which was probably one of the most far-reaching and influential battles in English military history? While ever ready to refer to and display its historical pedigree, the town also presents a vibrant modernity, offering a wide range of entertainment including music, theatre and festivals with no shortage of pubs, bars and restaurants. No doubt this eclectic range of amenities encourages the vast numbers of foreign students who choose to study here each summer, creating a lively cosmopolitan atmosphere about the town.

Being one of the original Cinque Ports, a maritime confederation dating back to the twelfth century, the town grew from its naval association into a strategically important harbour (originally situated where the lower parts of the town centre are today). Unfortunately, the topography was dramatically changed by silting and erosion, a common problem with this vulnerable coastline. This once natural harbour was to be abandoned by the end of the twelfth century, and by the thirteenth even its defensive Norman castle, built high up on a promontory above the harbour, had fallen prey to the inevitable landslips. On the West Hill are the remains of the first castle that William the Conqueror built in England.

Little of the old Hastings remains: a great deal was lost to the ravages of storms eating into the soft sandstone of the Weald (a thought for future climate change) and more lost to the ravages of the French. Today the area known as the Old Town lies between the two ridges of East Hill and West Hill presenting a close, comfortable ambience of enduring nostalgia where antique and small gallery shops nestle alongside old-fashioned pubs.

Whereas Brighton evolved as a major resort during the Regency period Hastings was more a creation of the Victorians. Although prompted by that period, its tentative Regency development had nothing of the vivacity of Brighton at the time. The real charm of Hastings is manifest in the timber-framed houses of the Old Town, with gabled roofs and raised pavements and bow-windowed Georgian houses, creating a wonderful mix of differing styles, often linked by quaint alleyways known locally as 'twitters'. To the western edge of the town we come to St Leonards, a little more self conscious and sedate, perhaps even slightly remote. Here the mix of architecture is a shade more controversial. Whatever one's taste in architecture it is worth ascending one of the hills, particularly the East Hill, on foot or by lift, for the striking view across the valley – here is Hastings at its best with past and present rolled into one.

BEXHILL-ON-SEA

My knowledge of Bexhill was limited to knowing that it proudly boasted a pavilion of sorts. It proved to be a plethora of surprises, not the least being when I first arrived to photograph the famous pavilion, only to find it covered in scaffolding and accompanied by the statement that it was 'due to be completed sometime in the summer of 2005'.

Less tiresome was the surprising fact that this quiet, if not conservative, seaside resort with its air of Edwardian propriety was the first place in the country to allow mixed bathing. Also, the building that I couldn't photograph (more scaffolding than building) was the first welded steel-framed building to be erected in England, and Bexhill was the first place in the country to stage formal auto-racing. In May 1902 the 8th Earl de la Warr negotiated with the Auto Club of Great Britain and Ireland to organise the event in the town. People flocked to the area in their thousands to watch the event – cars were to be travelling in excess of 50 mph, when the current speed limit was 12 mph. If this was not accolade enough, it was along the foreshore at Bexhill that the footprint of a 120 million-year-old iguanodon was recently (relatively speaking) found.

Much of the development of Bexhill, in particular the eponymous pavilion, was inspired by the 9th Earl de la Warr, who in 1932 became the town's first socialist mayor, advocated that if the pavilion was to be built it must be funded with public money, saying 'My view is that if it is going to pay private enterprise it is going to pay the town'. Good solid socialist reasoning indeed!

The clock tower on Bexhill seafront looking a little severe in the early morning. It was originally intended to commemorate the coronation of King Edward VII in 1902 but was not completed until 1904 – two years late is not the best of recommendations for a timepiece.

There was considerable public demand for a pavilion or entertainment site to be provided for the residents of Bexhill during the early years of the twentieth century. In 1910 the Central Parade was opened and was followed in 1911 by the Colonnade. These improvements to the town were very much welcomed, although they proved to be barely adequate. It was in April 1933 that the 9th Earl de la Warr proposed a scheme for an enclosed pavilion to be built behind the Colonnade – to which, of course, he gave his name.

The Colonnade was erected in the same year at George V's coronation, 1911. The building was designed by the architect J.B. Wall FRIBA.

It was a long time coming, but worth the wait! The newly restored, refurbished, facelifted de la Warr Pavilion is once again the splendid centrepiece to the Bexhill seafront that it had been in the past. Its champion, the 9th Earl de la Warr, would surely consider his vision and resolute efforts worthwhile were he to take a stroll along the shoreline today.

This newly resurrected Modernist building houses two art galleries, a café and restaurant as well as the main concert hall. The whole project has successfully transformed what was the first welded steel-framed building in the country back to its former pristine glory.

Opposite: The Pavilion's light, open interiors naturally evoke the sparkling moderne look of the art deco period.

Looking westwards from Hastings towards St Leonards one is confronted with what appears to be the stern-end view of a transatlantic liner; of course that is what we are meant to believe. Marine Court was one of the largest blocks of flats in England when it was completed just prior to the Second World War; an unheard-of thirteen storeys, and accompanied by the inevitable controversy. What the photograph does not show is the rest of the Marina to the west with its charming houses and buildings with classical façades and Ionic columns. I have to admit to having a soft spot for the thirteen-storey liner.

Opposite: Just a slight swell makes a dramatic scene on what is left of the old harbour wall at Hastings. It is no longer a viable harbour, so the local fleet fish directly from the beach, hauling their boats on to the shore with power-driven capstans. Meanwhile the locals soak up the rays!

When thinking of towns that are renowned for their architectural interest and splendour, Hastings does not immediately leap to the forefront of your mind. However, the seafront does have an arresting array of unusual buildings that give it a singular charm. This photograph of the Palace Court along the seafront is a fine example of what I mean, displaying an almost gothic stance. One wonders whether such a fragile chimney stack would ever be built today.

This quintet of craft on Hastings beach looked marvellously efficient and business like, obviously proud of their clean neat lines and regimented order, as though it were their duty to defend the beach head from imagined invaders.

Piers were an integral part of the development of a nineteenth-century seaside resort. Hastings pier was opened in 1872 by Earl Granville to immediate acclaim and success, which seems to have lasted right up until today. Designed by Eugenius Birch and modelled on the West Pier at Brighton, it incorporated an elegant, oriental-style pavilion at its southern end that was capable of seating some 2,000 people. It acquired further buildings during the next two decades. Misfortune struck on 15 July 1917 when the pavilion was destroyed by fire. Its replacement lacked the vigorous flamboyance of the original, but nevertheless provided a wealth of variety and entertainment through the 1920s and '30s, even to the extent of providing a searchlight to give those intrepid gay young things the chance of a swim at midnight. Naturally, activities were put on hold during the war years, but later the pier resumed its role, which it continues to play up to the present day.

These imposing weather-boarded net drying sheds with their neat gabled roofs are unique to Britain. The ones we see standing today at the east end of Hastings beach are probably no more than 150 years old, although the earliest examples are thought to date back to Tudor times. Most are still in use, and judging by their condition they are clearly monitored by the conservationists. One can even buy freshly caught fish at several stalls tucked away between the sheds.

This page and opposite: The East Hill lift at Hastings is reputedly the steepest railway track in Britain – looking at the photographs that fact is not too difficult to believe. The 22ft wide track that is 265ft in length was finished in spring 1902 at a cost of £6,000. Excavation work provided jobs for a good many local men, and the Grand Opening was set for 9 April, Coronation Day.

Originally the lift was water balanced, a decision that had been influenced by the plentiful supply of water nearby. Inside the two towers at the top of the lift were iron tanks, each capable of holding 1,200 gallons of water. Beneath the carriages were water tanks that could be filled from stand pipes by accessing the supply from inside the towers. Once enough weight had been gained by the upper of the two carriages to overcome the weight and inertia of the lower car the change-over of positions began. When the descending car arrived at the bottom the water in its tank was discharged and eventually pumped back up to the top.

The lift has remained popular as a tourist attraction. A modernising project in the 1970s saw the water balance method replaced by an electric motor. The overhaul cost around £35,000 and the lift reopened in 1976. The lift continues to be a success today, taking passengers to the cliff top to enjoy the spectacular views or perhaps visit the 600 acres of Hastings Country Park beyond.

A view from the Hastings Country Park down to the shore line where there is obvious evidence of previous cliff fall. As I write there is news of further slips along this section of the coastline and houses having to be abandoned. Much of the park is designated a Site of Special Scientific Interest. Formed in 1974, it covers some 540 acres of sandstone cliffs, picturesque glens covered by gorse and trees and a network of nature trails set out with picnic areas.

Much of the coastline between Pett Level and Hastings has undergone an almost constant series of minor changes and mishaps, sometimes not so minor. If it's not slips it's erosion and even quite dangerous rock falls, so it's always necessary to be on one's guard when exploring the shoreline and always be conscious of the state of the tide. This photograph was taken at the base of the cliff just west of Cliff End; the amazing stratification is like the grain of a piece of wood that has been cut lengthways.

This beautifully patterned slab of sandstone was found along the shoreline between Pett and Fairlight Cove. The markings may be impressions of fossils or a veneer of etchings created by time and sea. Here, if one is lucky, it is possible to find the casts of dinosaur footprints left in the sandstone beds. Recent studies by palaeontologists suggest that tracks of the iguanodons found in this area indicate that the creatures could have been up to 23ft in length and have weighed over 3 tons. If by some chance miracle the creatures should walk again there is no need to worry – these colossi were dedicated herbivores.

What you see is what you get – these distinct lines of stratification in the cliff face near Cliff End are not afraid to put their past on display; history is stripped naked and exposed for the world to see – the world being mostly gulls and jackdaws and a few intrepids who brave the possibility of rock falls at low tides. The white cliff makes a wonderful site with its thatch of obdurate foliage leaning tentatively away from the prevailing wind.

This photograph taken near Cliff End looks like the countryside of the Yosemite National Park in the United States.

Chapter Six

RYE & WINCHELSEA

RYE

Rye was once an island; now it is situated on its lofty perch between three rivers, the Rother, Brede and Tillingham, yet still today it has that physical aura of insularity. The layout of the town is unequivocally arranged on two levels: the Strand Quay leading to the much diminished harbour facilities, brought about by centuries of silting up at the river mouth, and the splendid, fortified bastion that constitutes the town centre. The two are linked by steeply cobbled lanes and alleyways or vertiginous flights of steps that echo its defensive past.

The town oozes history from every pore. Each piece of stonework looks as though it has escaped from a museum, but to its credit the town has not suffered from a surfeit of over-enthusiastic restoration. It has mostly resisted the temptation to 'bijouterie' or addiction to 'kitsch', save for perhaps the forgivable exception of the Strand redevelopment, which was once an area of old-fashioned wharf-side warehouses and now has a more picture postcard image.

Not only a historic gem but a cultural centre for the surrounding marsh and countryside, Rye organises two arts festivals a year, one in January and the other in September. The town art gallery consists of two buildings, one catering for exhibitions and sales of work by local artists and the other housing a permanent display of nineteenth- and twentieth-century British art. Its literary associations are many, the most famous being the connection with Henry James and his home at Lamb House. It also manages to service and supply the widespread and dependent communities of Romney Marsh to the east and the Weald to the north. If this were not enough, it also successfully caters throughout the year for armies of tourists, which must sometimes appear to the residents to be more daunting than the invading armies of previous centuries.

To the south of the town at the mouth of the river lies Rye Harbour village and the Rye Harbour Nature Reserve. This unique area of shingle and salt marsh is a mecca for birdwatchers and walkers alike. Management for the general area falls under the auspices of the Environment Agency. Much of the work on the nature reserve is undertaken by 'friends' – mostly volunteers – who staff and operate an efficient information centre from the quaint Lime Kiln Cottage close to the harbour entrance.

One of Rye's more eminent detractors has to be Jonathan Raban, who in his book *Coasting* chose to administer a verbal strafing on the town. While there is perhaps meagre justification for his criticism I rather think that he was trying to outdo his rival arch-cynic Paul Theroux and chose Rye to show off a bit. Rye is a time warp trapped in a fragile bubble of historic ether – and long may it remain so.

WINCHELSEA

As I mentioned in the introduction, I have counted Winchelsea as an honorary member of the Sussex coastline – just as celebrities may be granted an honorary degree at a university. Old Winchelsea (probably lying beneath Camber Sands in Rye Bay), having suffered continuous damage and encroachment by the sea, was eventually made uninhabitable by the great storm of 1287.

As one of the major English ports during the Middle Ages, its strategic importance was second to none, prompting Edward I to commission plans for a new town to be built to the north to replace vital harbour facilities. This town was to be built on Iham Hill, in those days a cliff promontory of seemingly invincible location with regard to the treacherous elements. However, it was not the invasion of the sea that was to prove the new town's downfall but its disappearance – the estuary soon began to silt up, and by the sixteenth century Winchelsea was no longer accessible by ship. The town was later to become as we know it today, high and dry.

A grid system of streets was incorporated in Edward's commission for the new town, an ambitious design of rigidity that has no comparison anywhere in England and is still just as much in evidence today as it was when it was first built. Today the wide verticals and horizontals of the street layout are graced with a certain charm that is enhanced by the mixture of medieval, Georgian, Victorian and more modern dwellings. Visitors to the town will find much evidence of and reference to its past inhabitants, be they fishermen, pirates or more sophisticated celebrities such as Dame Ellen Terry, the famous actress, or Vera Atkin, spy controller for SOE during the Second World War and the supposed model for Miss Moneypenny in Ian Fleming's Bond novels.

Five thousand years ago when the sea level was considerably lower Pett shore would have been covered in forest. The remains of this oak forest, blackened stumps, can be seen today when the tide is out. These amazing prehistoric relics litter the shoreline looking like half-submerged pieces of a forgotten shipwreck. To touch them and realise their age at the same time is something of a mindblowing exercise.

The Church of St Thomas the Martyr. This serenely beautiful building quietly dominates the town of Winchelsea. After the destruction of the old Winchelsea Edward I was determined to build the new town and port on higher and safer ground, not only as a precaution against the ravages of the sea but as a more strategically defensive harbour against foreign invasion. The new town was to be built on a modern system incorporating the principle of the grid and its church was to be one of the most magnificent in the land. The original building was planned as much larger than we see it today, employing the most skilled stonemasons in the country.

Sussex oak was used for the timber rafters, some of which can be seen after 700 years. Stone was brought from Caen in Normandy and marble was quarried in Sussex for the interior. Effigies in black marble lie in medieval tombs: they are believed to have been salvaged from the old church. The works of Douglas Strachan (1875–1950), an artist in stained glass, dominate the walls in a memorial to those who fell in the First World War as well as those who died defending the Cinque Ports. Touchingly, over the sedilia in the south wall is a stained-glass memorial commemorating the bravery of the crew of the *Mary Stanford* who so tragically lost their lives in 1928.

love light peace
terence alan
(spike)
milligan c.b.e., k.b.e.
1918 - 2002
grá mhór ort shelagh
writer • artist • musician
humanitarian • comedian
dúirt mé leat go raibh mé breoite
loving father
laura • sean • • jane
eternally loved by his grandchildren

Setting up for a day's fishing on Winchelsea beach. Dungeness Power Station can just be seen in the far distance.

Opposite: Hilarious, complex, eccentric, all adjectives that have been used at various times to describe the unpredictable Spike Milligan. Even after his death the same descriptions prevail, for on his gravestone in the graveyard of Winchelsea church there is a short epitaph inscribed in Gaelic. It simply translates as 'I told you I was ill'.

It was thought that the building of the sea wall behind Winchelsea beach would make the numerous groynes redundant. Presumably that idea succeeded for a while, for the incumbent structures were left to the vicissitudes of time and tide. However, judging by the work going on in this photograph we are back to readdressing the problem using the original method.

Camber Castle stands 1½ miles from the shore amid fields of grazing sheep and watery salt marsh, its nearest neighbour a bird-watching hide on the quiet waters of the nature reserve. Instigated by Henry VIII as a coastal defence against possible invasion from Europe, the building work began in 1539. However, owing to the changing topography of the area, caused by the build-up of shingle, it had to be abandoned in 1642. Its design is the same as the castles at Deal, Walmer, Sandgate and Sandown, the perimeter a footprint exactly representing the shape of the Tudor Rose. Today it relaxes in comfortable isolation and is only accessible on foot. From its silent walls grow the wall pennywort, the wall pepper and the pellitory-of-the-wall. There are several watercolours of the castle by the war artist Paul Nash who lived in the area at one time.

This page and opposite: The Church of St Mary dominates the centre of the town of Rye, rising above the Ypres Tower and looking out towards the sea and across Romney Marsh. It encourages a quiet tranquillity amid the often crowded and bustling lanes that make up the rest of the town. It rests in a dignified close of medieval houses that provide a historic heart to the town and a much recognised landmark for miles around. The clock, which has become a tourist attraction in its own right, has an eighteenth-century surround and model boys to strike the quarter hour (quarter boys). The whole piece is driven by a sixteenth-century mechanism, which is one of the oldest still working in England. The two photographs opposite were taken from the top of the church tower.

The Ypres Tower is the oldest building in Rye open to the public, presenting splendid views over the harbour and surrounding countryside. Next door is a comfortable pub called the Ypres Castle Arms (opposite) – so if the chequered history of the tower is a little challenging, one can always take consolation in a pint! The outline of the building has not changed in over 700 years. This miniature castle was built in 1249, its sturdy, squat design with three quarter round towers saw little active service, and by 1430 was being used by John de Ypres as living accommodation. By 1518 it had become a prison, a function that it maintained until the 1860s. In 1870 an extension was built to its northern elevation to provide a soup kitchen for the poor and needy during a particularly harsh winter. By the end of the century the ground floor had been converted into a mortuary, a service performed well into the next century. In 1942 a German air raid badly damaged the red-tile roof causing it to be demolished. In 1954 it was opened as the Rye Museum, housing a collection of many items associated with the town's history.

The Ypres Castle Arms, Rye.

No longer the busy commercial quayside that it once was, Rye is still subjected to high tides, especially spring tides, that often cause flooding across the road. In this photograph the boats are not far off being level with the roadside, the A259, and it can seem quite eerie to look out of the car window and see a motor launch on the same plane.

Opposite: One of the many picturesque lanes to be found in Rye. The town abounds in narrow, cobbled streets and alleys, often brimming with pots and containers full of brightly coloured flowers and shrubs during the summer months.

This page and opposite: These ancient-looking sea defences at Rye Harbour were probably built after the serious flooding in 1926. Today they have almost become beach sculptures: their worn and moulded forms certainly would not look out of place at the Turner Prize, and would most likely be a welcome improvement. Close by stands the deserted lifeboat house that once held the *Mary Stanford* and her tragically haunting memories. Soon after 5 a.m. on 15 November 1928 the maroon went up, calling the crew to lifeboat duty. They and many who were to help in a hazardous launch staggered from their beds out into a pitch black and angry night. Scrambling across a darkened beach and fields opposed by gale-force winds and driving rain, many must have felt exhausted before reaching the boathouse. Confronted by the situation of a tide at its lowest ebb and a lifeboat that had to be hauled well over half a mile to the water's edge, following two dangerous and abortive attempts to launch they were finally successful on the third occasion; all they had to do now was to haul up the sail, man the oars and disappear into a night of enormous seas and terrifying conditions. This was a bravery and commitment to saving the lives of others that was without limits.

THAT WHICH WAS
HERBERT HEAD
HENRY CUTTING

Between the quayside and Rye Harbour mouth it is possible to find any number of interesting boats in various states of renovation or undergoing maintenance and repair by committed enthusiasts and professionals alike, and often an artist with paint and easel capturing the event for posterity.

Opposite: The lifeboat memorial in the Rye Harbour churchyard dedicated to the crew of the *Mary Stanford*. There will never be a true answer, only speculation, as to what happened in the hours between the lifeboat being launched and her capsizing on that fateful and tragic night, as none of the crew lived to tell the tale.

Rye bay is notorious for storms across her waters. In one such storm in the early hours of the morning of 15 November 1928 a Latvian ship, *Alice of Riga*, and a German steamer, the *Smyrna*, collided in horrendous seas south-west of Dungeness. The captain of the German ship radioed that the *Alice* had been holed and was taking in water and drifting out of control. The message was relayed to Rye Harbour coastguard station and the *Mary Stanford* was launched in the most desperate and abominable weather conditions. Seventeen brave men were never to return to their community.

This page and opposite: Several beach sculptures remain from what was a sculptural walk project initiated in 2003 at the mouth of Rye Harbour. Various artists have created works that interpret and engage with man's association with nature, often making use of materials found on the beach and along the sea shore. It is even possible to view these sculptures from the comfort of the Lime Kiln Cottage Information Centre by using a touch screen video terminal, along with a wealth of other information that the centre provides.

This page and opposite: Used by the Romans for exporting iron, Rye Harbour was also a major strategic port during the Middle Ages. However, silting and the creation of sand bars prevented larger draft shipping from entering the harbour, although regular dredging has enabled smaller commercial shipping to still use the wharf facilities. Now the harbour is used mainly by the fishing fleet and a thriving yachting community. Today the harbour is maintained and administered by the Environment Agency.

There is something resolute and infinite about the Old Watch House at the end of Rye Harbour – perhaps it's the pitch black solidness that defies anything with a whiff of impermanence. Much like the fishermen's houses that you find out on the Dungeness Point, they have a look of having been there forever and the intention of staying a whole lot longer. As with other forms of architecture the style has its appeal and ardent admirers, one of whom recently had a seaside dwelling built at Dungeness resembling one such fishermen's hut – the low steel-frame construction was cocooned in a dense black rubber material to give it a 'natural' tarred appearance. Nothing is too much trouble for pseudo authenticity!

Scots Float – the sluice and tidal limit of the River Rother.

One of the many ditches that drain the surrounding marshland near Scots Float – this particular one displaying a quite magnificent reed bed that is so typical of the area and provides a haven for water birds and bank-side creatures. The reed beds' elegant forms are often bathed in a golden light.

St Mary's Church at East Guldeford is unusual in a couple of ways: its construction in brick and its twin-roof design, with the bell cote situated between the two pitches, which gives it more the appearance of a barn than an ecclesiastical building. It sits in a field just off the A259, an extremely narrow piece of road between two bends. To access it from the road is to risk life and limb, as there is little or no room at the road's edge and lorries hurtle past with total disregard for human life. It has a very pleasant graveyard, though! Incidentally, I reached the church from the Camber Road, crossing several fields and dykes with hidden bridges before getting there, but it was well worth the effort to see this hidden gem. The church was built by Sir Richard de Guldeford in 1505 and now supported by the Romney Marsh Historical Churches Trust.

The low tide has left a patchwork of sand bars and pools almost as far as the eye can see across this unrelentingly flat landscape, looking west from Camber to the Rye Harbour arm in the distance. It is difficult to imagine from this tranquil photograph of the harbour mouth that the tides that race through the bay can be deadly and dangerous.

Camber Sands is several miles of sand flats stretching from the edge of Lydd ranges to the eastern border of Rye Harbour. The tide here seems to go out forever – horse riders beside the sea appear on the horizon as if in a distant landscape, and at low tide you will walk for what seems miles before reaching the water's edge, then miles again through warm sandy water before it reaches your waist. Naturally, it is very popular with visiting families during the summer months because of the miles of space and sand. Even when the tide is high the dunes on its northern edge offer a safe adventure playground for the young. Evidence of its popularity can be seen in this photograph; a line of sentinel-like litter bins quietly wait to devour new volumes of holiday rubbish.

This page and opposite: The dunes at Camber, like many areas along the south coast, are subject to sand migration. By using chestnut fencing staked across their breadth it is possible to considerably reduce this disappearance as well as help to create wonderfully sculpted images in an ever-changing random design.

A TV crew filming on the beach at Camber.

When the children have returned to school and most visitors have gone it is possible once more to appreciate the wild spatial beauty of the place. However, one late summer visitor caused a considerable stir. The *Maanav Star*, a 2,000 ton Indian freighter, unable to hold her own in a fierce storm, was blown up on to the beach at Camber and well and truly grounded. Allegedly without sufficient ballast she was tossed up on to the beach like a piece of flotsam, during fierce weather conditions. When I arrived to take photographs the storm was still raging and only the police and coastguard were warily monitoring the scene. Within an hour several more photographers had arrived and like myself, battling against a slicingly bitter wind and sea spray, attempted to capture the moment.

Note on the Photographs

Many people find talk of cameras, lenses and film profoundly boring, and indeed the technical facets of photography can often detract from the impact and spontaneity when first looking at an image. Most photographers are not bored by the inclusion of technical data, to the extent that there is a need-to-know attitude concerning the way in which a particular image has been created and formed. With some it borders on the obsessional.

I have no intention of filling pages with f. stop numbers or shutter speed times, but will take the opportunity to list the materials that I used and give a brief insight into my approach to the project. If you happen to be one of the profoundly bored you should skip to the next page.

While I have made fairly liberal use of a medium format camera (Mamiya 645) for landscape shots, its use has by no means been exclusive; many of the shots have been taken on 35mm, namely an Olympus OM2, Olympus XA and a Nikon F70. I have no single preference for film, using Ilford FP4 and HP5, Fuji Neopan 100 and 400, Kodak T.MAX 100 and 400, developed in Ilford film developer or Agfa Rodinal. The photographic papers for this publication included Ilford Multigrade IV, Barclay Poly-Grade and Adox – mostly developed in Spur paper developer; this developer seems to keep forever in the tray.

The use of black and white film allows the eye to seek out and explore detail; whereas colour, no matter how good the composition or how rich the hues, is a kaleidoscope that merely encourages the eye to jump from one area to another across the surface of the print. The use of colour takes the eye into a scene; through it; out again as if the image is transparent – with black and white the eye lingers, held by small mysteries that enthral in the same way that a *noir* movie does.

In the end it is down to engaging with what is there in front of you. And with a little luck the light will be half reasonable and the incoming tide not about to envelop you. This journey along the Sussex coast was enjoyable and I often savour many of the visual experiences that I remember – hopefully they will hold some relevance for the reader.

INDEX